D0924586

Wind picks up, leaves flutter and swirl
the grace you etched with your turns and twirls
will remain for a long long time.

Chris

POEMS BY
BRUCE
FESSENDEN

TEMPLE DANCER

Doesn't it get old sometimes?
That repetition of the same?
That slow drip of karma
   bones of antelope and deer
  mud hole dust
   brown and brittle grasses
   flutter in the twilight wind.

Blue, blond; you work your channels
   At ease with yourself
   you write your flowing script.
Beat of wings, ancient rituals and prayers.
Warm air, shorebirds floating
   waves crash the central California coast.
Pebble beach, redwoods fill the ravines
   high above, on a golden overlook
   a temple: open air, columns of granite, marble floor.
Ritual dancing, the maidens pause
   silk tunics billow in the wind
   rose petals float in the air
Sun-splashed and briney
   silence of the afternoon
   inhale, pause for an instant
   exhale.

For you are an old beauty, my dear
   the Czarist palace extravagant
   yet smokey and tainted with mold
   smaller than you remembered it.
The others ran, while you remained in your room

kept teaching your classes
even when just the old ones showed up
even with the blood on the floor
you offer what you can.
A carriage was waiting for you, my dear
with a different name, official passport
yet you stayed behind.
Wind picks up, leaves flutter and swirl
the grace you etched with your turns and twirls
will remain for a long long time.

Water running black, under the ice
summertime tree forever slim and strong
even when they turned off your light.
Scavenge for crumbs, and give praise for the blossoms
even then your boat floated straight.
Trumpets still sounding
falcons still soaring
there will always be a stitch in the sacred fabric
even if you never come back.

It had to be done
pull of the future
with all that tearing, all that loss
but you, you still sit on the throne
they will never touch you.
You never learned the language or the ways
you were too proud for that.
You never forgot who you were
you never abandoned hope.
Palace up on the bluff
views across the river and its steady currents
languid, like your waltz turns

you never became corrupted
you never needed to change.

They took your bracelets and jewelry, they threw me in jail
    but I kept your little cedar box.
And I read and re-read the letters you wrote
    to officials, family, lieutenants and commanders
    tide shifting suddenly, aristocracy alarmed
    terrified
    blood everywhere
    instruments heavy and blunt.
Your council steady and true
    in the end it wasn't enough.

The sacrifice was made on the springtime equinox
    dawn's earliest light.
Three days of fasting, praying all night.
She was the prettiest, still a girl
    blond, blue eyed
    clear and strong in word and thought.
In an open air temple
    on a bluff overlooking the Pacific
    her swan like neck on a marble block
    the axe heavy and sharp.

And who wields the axe?
Who lifts that heavy blade?
The blade is lifted even now
    hairs tingle at the back of your neck.
You can peel away the husk
    but you might not want to see her face.

SILVER AND GOLD

Could be anyone:
doctor or lawyer, beggerman, that man over there
in the silver Benz—
probably works in commercial real estate.
Could be anyone:
stranger, child, mayor—
when you walk through the door
    you walk alone.

It's a tourist town; the old church looks out of place—
    made in the olden ways: adobe, stucco, rough-hewn pine.
Massive door, iron hinges heated and hammered:
    craftsman's long dead, but what he wrought lives on.
Lilies with elongated stems intertwined
  etched into the hinges, carved in the wood.
Door creaks when opened, yet it's well balanced—
 swings easily in spite of the weight.
Air inside is cool and musty. When you breathe,
    your body relaxes.
I have no idea why.

Patterns in the wood, enhanced with stains.
    Your pattern is a little more hidden.
You're the queen of our second-hand store:
you reign over the patchwork quilts, the musty old books,
    used Barbie dolls with broken limbs and glass eyes.
You stopped eating years ago and I worry so.
    Hard to get your nourishment
    when you're living only on light.
Regal yet funny, your cup's always filled.

You never plan ahead; you have another glass of wine.
You have faith the land will provide.

You plowed the earth, hammered the silver;
you said you weren't much of a craftsman—
you did better than you think.
You composed our garden with your suffering.
    Such a small plot.
I suppose a well-balanced door can swing both ways.
You sold your pearls to save your kingdom—
you already reserved your little white room
in the other world, over on the other side.

Old church sandwiched between mini mall and apartment building—
    the sacred often found nested within the ordinary.
Light turns green, tourists rush by.
    For many the church doesn't exist.
Wooden cross, cracked and dry,
bleached by the sun, held up by rusty wires
now slack and sagging from the passage of time.
    Yet the cross remains silently standing.

I thought I was depressed, but I was expanded.
    I curled up on your porch,
        hair clumped and matted.
I lost my homeland, my voice melted away.
    It was as if you were talking to my guardian angel.
  Is it because you'd already sacrificed yourself?
We talked about the weather, made silly little jokes—
the quilt of intimacy woven from minor details.
People like you safeguard the love—
        yours is the generosity of a fool.

It's always the final day with you—
the final hour, the final gesture.
Won't you please eat some food?
You need your nourishment; the world isn't ending just yet.
You are radiance and you are golden—
I suppose some must step aside
    before others can step up.
I'll clean your room if you put down your wine.
    No more purging—
you've purged enough.

They march through the old world village,
boots clomping on cobblestones,
    brass band playing slightly off key.
Marching through the fields, around the cemetery,
up the goat path and onto the ridge, beneath the afternoon sky.
Singing the whole time, they pause at the top
and begin to toss blossoms red and pink:
    dozens, hundreds, tens of thousands.
Driven by the wind, held by the silence,
the blossoms float out to the horizon
    and wink out.
Music plays on, twilight sky hardens into darkness
    like your past hardens inside your body.
We stay hidden, you and I, hidden like a couple of fugitives.
Yet the face of mercy is everywhere
    more hidden than us.

Better pack your socks, bring some eggs and cheese—
perhaps a craft of a good Italian wine.
You don't take anything, you trust the world,
    the grace you've accumulated
    you've tossed back to your friends.

I'll give you my quarters—I wish I had more.
Yours is the hardest path I've ever known.

I tried to pay for my life with my darkness—
    the most beautiful thing I own.
I'm that solitary figure working long hours in the forest.
    My chain is dull; saw making a racket—
    I never heard the humming of the angels.
You gave me your scarves
    and Alta-Tadema prints.
I held them for years
    but I never gave them away.

It's a hot afternoon, band playing in the plaza
    beneath the massive church door.
Trumpets and tubas, drums and accordion,
    the fiddle player looks battered
    looks like he could use a drink.
Brassy and melancholy, a little crooked,
    notes reverberate off the whitewashed walls.
Children stop their playing and grandmothers nod
    as the procession slides by.
Weddings and funerals, they look the same—
    a link with something unknowable.

Wolves prowl the high pasture, they stalk the lambs.
    Think I'll take some of the red blossoms,
    rub them into my sore.
Or build a fire, grind up some seeds,
    make a tea, drink it before bed.
They say love is everything, and I believe those words are true,
    but love is a slippery fish
    that keeps sliding through my nets.

I am haunted and you are strange.
    I'd like to think
       our common denominator is sacred mystery,
       but I fear its something darker.

There's a time for beginnings and a time for endings,
like the moment I had my first breakdown.
Dad's violence leaking into my body,
      my world reconfigured forever.
Or when you had your first drink
or first heard Mahler—
      fireworks filled your sky,
      your body filled with song.
It's one step forward and two steps back—
who can say which is the preferred way?
If I wasn't so raw, my senses wouldn't wick up the starlight;
     songs of the whales sounding over lavender waters
     wouldn't seep through the cracks in my head.

You better pack some instruments: a compass or a map,
     a sextant for reading the stars.
You think you need nothing; you might be right—
I know you're at ease in the invisible land.
But your boat is so small,
     still waters black and cold—
     human senses are warped in that eerie half-light.
Just a crown of flowers and some tossed off regrets.
     Your footprints are fading,
     but the light in your heart shows you the way.

My fear is a piece of the mosaic,
     a turn in the labyrinth,
     the bruise on the apple.

What did I bring you, anyway—
    you who are more hidden than I?
You walked through this land,
     your wicker basket filled with red flowers,
     wolves licking your hand.

I broke my back because I fell too far.
I never should have set foot in this world.
I am the misshapen cavity;
I am the resonant pit nobody ever noticed;
I am the lumpy stranger singing the song
     nobody ever forgets.
The world is careless now, yet the fruit has ripened,
     ready for the taking.

Everything you did, everything you could have been—
parents and grandparents, obstacles, triumphs—
    all that was just loaned to you.
Loaned to you by the world;
    now its time to give it back.
I paid you in silver—I wish I paid you in gold.
    What's done is done.
all that remains is the Nocturne, the Slow Masurka.
You're slipping away, but your dances live on—
     your dances belong to God.

Confusion reigns:
red blossoms dropping from the palms
    of the angels outspread hands,
They're copying you,

but they can't match your ease
or your grace.
They thought you were one of them.
The angels look up to you—
follow you around.
They can only experience life
through your sacred particularity.
You keep forgetting the door swings both ways.

MARGARET JENKINS PERFORMANCE
Part One

This is a time of tearing
   the animals have all run to higher ground
   while humans stumble about, in random arcs collapsing in on
   themselves
   then falling darkly down.
It's funny, words don't count for much anymore
   nobody reads, everyone looking for something to sell.
But my dear, you always stood tall
   perhaps you are way ahead of the rest of us
   for you don't say anything at all
   except 'no', to the food the nurse brings you
   you ask if there's any dessert.
When the nurse leaves you say to me
   'I keep telling them I don't eat meat'.

I'll never untangle the mystery that is you
   neither word nor story that I piece together
   can possibly ring true
   you hide your face inside conflict and enigma.
But the Margaret Jenkins performance was
   a stone of starlight, sparkling in the grass
   a shy and chaste flower, every year blossoming more beautiful
   my dear, that was your finest hour.
At the Margaret Jenkins Studio, almost 40 years ago now, 1982
   mid-January, a few days after my birthday
   one of the rainiest winters on record.

                                             ☙

I was so tired that night
   sometimes I think it's my dreams
   that awaken the fatigue in my bones.
I was selling firewood then
   we had absolutely no money
   doing what I could to keep our dreams alive
   half the time my pick-up wouldn't start.
I was in San Francisco that day, making a delivery
   to a rich person, who wanted me
   to carry the wood through his house
   stack it on his back porch.
Told me I could take it or leave it
   stack it where he wants it, or
   he's not going to pay for the wood.

Cord of oak weighs almost 4000 pounds, even if fully dried.
That's 50 trips to the asshole's back porch
   even if I carry 80 pounds per trip
   or a 100 trips if I carry 40 pounds
   I'm just a slave, you might as well lynch me.
My cotton hoodie soaking up the rain
   I can see my breath on this cold winter day.

Margaret Jenkins Studio in the Mission District
   a rough and rowdy neighborhood before gentrification
   someone might pull a pistol on me as I walk to the theater
   I carried a piece of oak, just to be safe.
If a problem should arise, I'd bash the perpetrator upside the head.
Had $150 cash in my wallet, payment for the firewood delivery
   easily one months rent.

Shivering cold as I approach the theater
   you could wring rainwater out of my socks.

People milling about, outside the theater
    relaxed and confident, wearing expensive clothes.
I'm deep inside my impenetrable tar
    as I crack open the theater door, slip on through.
I'm lumpy and awkward, my tee shirt ripped and torn
    I don't belong here, I'll hide in a corner
    It'll all be over before too long.

∾

Because I'm receptive, the child in me easily shifts
    or perhaps the grief inside my bulky darkness
    has been starving for even a suggestion of a fresh breeze.
Inside there's a buzz of anticipation
    it's a festive mood, and I quickly catch that wave.
The place is packed, 300 seats the theater holds
    both nights long since sold out.
The bohemian crowd of San Francisco on full display
    dancers, poets, mimes, gypsies
    as well as older people, many who had seen
    Isadora's adopted daughters dance in the 30s
    Irma, Maria-Theresa
    or even Isadora herself in the years before she died.

And because you are my partner
    many in attendance know me, know my name
    glass of champagne thrust in my hand.
Accepted, even welcomed, a balm to my feverish soul
    even as rainwater drips from my hoodie and Levi's
    puddles forming on the hardwood floors
    wherever I place my feet.

DIONYSIAN DUNCAN DANCERS

Performing Company of the Isadora Duncan International Institute of Classical Dance

present

DANCES FROM THE REPERTOIRE
OF ISADORA DUNCAN

JANUARY 22 & 23 at 8:30pm

Margaret Jenkins Performance Space
1590 15th Street (at Mission), San Francisco

Admission $5. - Reservations: 863-7580

3435 Army Street, Studio 204, San Francisco, California, 94110, (415) 282-9559

THE ANSWER TO LOVE IS DEATH

You, my dear
    with your sacred alter of self obliteration
    with your smooth skin and composed eyes
    you never wavered; your faithfulness unblemished –
    but you have lost your way.

What are you enchanted by? I can't even guess.
It's like you live in a room in a manor house
    on the outskirts of a European capital
    Prussia, or Czarist Russia, or Victorian London.
And you are titled, you still have a dribble of an income
    but you are the only one left.
It's winter now, there's frost on your walls
    the fire in your room has gone out
   you haven't eaten in three days
    and you don't even notice.

What does it mean to be perfect?
    Perfect in your solitude
    perfectly unmoving
    because you've given your stars away
    because you've bartered away your blood.
Are you closer to the angels now?
    Are you closer to the timeless?
Are you closer to that palace of perfection?
    Where there is no need for the spoken word
    because anything said would be a subtraction?
Who is the being of solitude
    holding you so sweetly, so tenderly?
It must be a lovely tune that she sings to you

a song the rest of us strain hard to hear.
Sounds of the celestial choir
with a script from the gilded tabernacle
a mesmerizing tune, sweetly whispered into your ear.

And now I shake your shoulder
    but you don't wake up, I shake again
    you say my name.
I ask if you want your scone, your coffee with foamed milk.
You nod, but still wordless, you roll over
    and I wonder who you are, and what you came here for
    and what it is I'm being given.

You said once, long ago
    that this planet —planet Earth
    is the love planet.
We come here to learn about love.
But my dear, love is connection, and you keep to yourself
    you don't reach out
    even as a child you were so still and quiet
    and I wonder again
    the source of your enchantment.

For it is through chanting and ritual
    that sacred space may be held.
And you always had that nimbus of sacred space about you
    even now, with your blankets over your head
    you seem complete.

Why the dried flowers, why the wilted tulips
    why the ghosts?
Why the five thousand days
    with the New York Times and your six glasses of wine

tucked away in a corner of your Solano Street restaurant
a silent ritual where nothing can change.
You live in a different realm
a realm of solitude, frozen time.
Who is singing to you, I wonder
who is the being that has captured your mind?

You should take some of your own advice
and spend a little time here on Earth.
Learn what you can about love –
a tricky and slippery subject
yet worth the struggle and effort.
Death can be more than a stasis or an endpoint.
The activity of death would serve you well
by breaking your endless ritual of wine and silence.
All that trapped love—wouldn't it be nice
for your love to find expression in the world?
This is a death that releases
This is a death that opens.

You sleep with the window open
your feet look like they're frozen.
You got some socks lying by your bed
I wish you would put them on.

Soup for Chris

You are mostly silence now, the fire is on the other side.
You are mostly the tree that looks different, the soup that doesn't
    smell right.
    And lately I've been having luminous dreams.

Like waiting, on a train platform.
    It looks like someplace in Europe
    only nobody is there.
    Just a few pigeons, doing pigeon things,

I feel the grief, it washes me clean
    washes off the dirt, and I am smaller.
You have already gone, and you will never save yourself.
    You are that brave.
    Blossoms from your basket hang in the air
    as I run to collect them.
    I keep thinking about order and direction
    I keep thinking there is a way through.
    You are way ahead of me, way more realistic.

The truth is in the brokenness.
    You finish yourself by being broken
    you finish yourself by being so small, almost infinitely small.
    Maybe only then can God see you.
    You had the courage to go all the way.
    You submitted completely.
I look at the train platform now
    and it is empty, except for the pigeons.
    The train is already gone.
    I will finish your soup, for I hate wasting food.

MARGARET JENKINS PERFORMANCE

Part Two

Isadora's intent with her dance was not the creation
    of an eye-catching artifact to be admired
    rather, her dance a communion with the spirits and angels
    a building of soul in the exchanging
    stitch by stitch, bead by bead
    the inner-ness of everyday life and the natural world linked
    for the Holy lives in everything.
Even a gesture as simple
    as serving a glass of milk
    can invoke the sacred.

As I am instantly linked with San Francisco's past
    upon entering the theater
    for the dances of Isadora like an animating pulse
    inside Ferlinghetti and Rexroth
    Ginsberg and Kerouac.
And the push for workers rights—
    a sanctifying of the common man
    played out on the streets of San Francisco in the 30s
    spirit of Isadora infused every piece of that.
Or the all night bacchanals of the Grateful Dead
    when the Dead were young and strong
    fueled by drugs of course
    but behind the drugs, a ferocious longing for transcendence
    yearning to go further, push deeper
    all the way to the end of time.
    Maybe then I'll catch a glimpse of God's face
    maybe then I'll find the path back to myself.

To dance Isadora's dances is to be lived by the Gods.
And as I write this I'm thinking that
    I should honor the awkward parts of myself
    for those are the parts where I will be sanctified
    where I am sanctified.
    My dense and mis-fitted parts, my everyday dirt—
    if I'm honest with myself I might understand
    that my awkwardness is the fertile soil of the collective dream
    waterfalls where the spirits gather
    sacred soil for the blossoming of kindness.

ANTICIPATING THE GOLDEN STAIRWAY

On your last day you say almost nothing
   no goodbyes, no final wishes
   a few tears, unusual for you, as queens are not weak like that
   queens should be above all that.

I drive you to the Rose Garden
we drink our coffee there.
I nibble at my scone, glance at the paper
you eat nothing, you just stare ahead. A foggy morning
you are transfixed; I wonder what you are seeing.
Liberation has found you
   finally, you are released from your debts.

We go home; you go straight to bed
   you don't say anything to me
   we've known each other for so long
   a language of silences now, and loss.
I read, but I'm too distracted to read
   I pray, but I'm too distracted to pray.
Death is the greatest intimacy
   a black hole
   your singularity, but also my singularity.
I will never be the same
   I am part of your whirlpool of extreme self-neglect
   and I walk the golden stairs.
At every moment, the stairs are mine
   the self-neglect is mine as well.

When I poke my head into your bedroom, you are gone.
Your face frozen, eyes frozen, staring ahead
   yet somehow, because it is you
   you look relaxed.
No problem for you leaving your body
   you always had so much courage.

Oh my dear, we are both failures.
We both picked the flowers of the strange narcotic.
We both wandered down the roads of loss, which go nowhere
   only circling back in a spiral of collapse.
I didn't give you my spark
   I gave you my dried leaves.
But you were already gone
You wandered out the back door, back to a country that never existed
   back to a place where promises are routinely broken
   and everyone wears masks.

Still, there is beauty, still there is the warmth of summer
   rose petals floating in the air
   seraphims of joy and harvest
   unseen presences in the background
   their hands stretched out, offering.
You didn't just know beauty, you were beauty
   because of that, you were also contamination
   later, rot.
You were never able to come to a place of protection.
You remained in the realm of the timeless
   a more dangerous place
   not out of fear, rather out of love.

I carry you from your bedroom into the living room
    lay you down on the couch.
The bedroom is a mess
    books and dance magazines and yellowing newspaper articles
    stacked clear to the ceiling.
Because your soul is frightened and confused, I stay with your body
    though I don't know how much direction I can provide.
I stay by you for two days, sitting in the wing chair
    before I call 911.
I pray to God, I beg for forgiveness, I pray to
    your Hungarian ancestors
    and I don't eat a thing.
I sit and weep, for both of us.

ON THE OTHER SIDE OF THE MOUNTAIN

I've never been to that enchanted land
   where people fly without wings.
Where truths of the heart are stamped into every blade of grass.
And temples of marble grace the golden hills
offering a view to the west, to the waters of the deep
   with the shorebirds, the foam, the salt.
Where immortal blood flows in the veins of those who live here
   it all collapses into a song
   into the familiar dream.

Oh I know I'll never get there
   and I know you never left.
Way down deep inside
   I hold a memory of that glow
   shining through the curtains of the unknown.
A land without shadows, where beauty lives uncorrupted
   where the hopes of the heart are already here
   and there are no tears
   there are no regrets.

I wanna go there, I wanna go home
I wanna go to that place where love is never tainted
where with every exchange I get exactly what I need
where I'm never in debt, and I never get cold
where I can give freely, where my timing is on cue
   you are an angel from that heavenly place.

It is the land of the Grail
   where all souls lived before the fall
      a land of milk and honey, without bitterness or strife
      where one deed flows into the next like a musical river
      every stitch a holy stitch
      every gesture forming the higher good.
Where wine is served in crystal goblets
      fresh fish served on platters of glass
      with garnish and herbs and slices of lemon.
Dessert is raspberries and fresh whipped cream
      served in little painted bowls from a country to the east
      silver spoons stamped with the sigil of the king.

There are no commoners here, bloodlines are pure
      no farts or belches, streets are pristine.
Every day is mid-summer, all wear tunics of silk
      when it rains, it's a festival of renewal
      every soul scrubbed bright and clean.

Oh my dear, it must be hard carrying the burden of perfection
      in spite of the weight of the corruptions and disappointments
      of this fallen world.
 You, more than anyone else I know
      maintain yourself in a sacred purity
      I don't know how you do it
      I suppose just by being you.
Even your faults, even your radical self neglect
      seem to come from a higher place.

Remember when we first met?
Still teenagers then
      so full of hope, so few regrets.

Spring of '67, we went to the places your family went
    up Highway 1, to the lost coast
    to the redwood parks, to Russian Gulch.
Fifty years have passed since I last visited Mendocino
    don't think I'll go there without you
    for me, it would just be a place of absence now
    it would just be another touristy place.

But then, for the majority of your adult life
that seemed to be what you were doing
You connect with yourself through self-abandonment.
Just a maiden floating in a little wooden boat
    floating on the wide, wine dark sea.
    Just drifting out to the horizon, shaped by the elements
    all the way out to infinity.
Out to where all things in this world have their beginnings
    the place where they have their endings too.
Smell of salt, warm August sun
    are the white doves leading you on
    or are they following you?
Asters and lilies fill your footsteps
    distant trumpets announce your coming.
Banners swirl and unfurl in the summertime air.
The mother of God, the source of all things
here comes the Queen!
gracing a world without shadow
every heart's golden dream.

Out there in your boat, floating with the tides
    out to the horizon, out to the other side
    out there, where all things are complete unto themselves
    even words are unnecessary
    any word spoken would be a subtraction.

Out there in your boat, filled with every good intention
    there are no distractions here, and not much wind
    so much peace and tranquility
    that even the gods have left.

We went back to my apartment that night we met
    fooled around a bit
    listened to the Rolling Stones, 12x5.
You said you liked that raunchy sound
    you said you liked the blues.
But my dear, after fifty years
    I still don't see much blue in you.
    You who suffer more deeply than any one
    even your suffering is perfect.

BEIGE TRENCH COAT

Every moment of your past is still here
Every moment of your past a stitch in the invisible fabric.
It is your offering, your lived life, a precious lavender bead
      now given back.

Even the moments that didn't happen, but
could have happened are here.
You easily could have been the dance critic for the Chronicle.
With your encyclopedic knowledge of everything ballet
      I wish I'd recorded your thoughts.
Even after your decline, your perfect nature remains in the world
like a lavender prayer bead, or a rose embossed cross.

I rummage through your piles of clothes
milk cartons filled with clothes, and wicker baskets
you never would hang them or fold them.
A chaotic welter, pieces of you scattered about haphazardly,
      like crumbs
and because of that, parts of myself that I've mislaid all these years
      like your denim jacket, size extra small
      delicate embroidery down the front
      did you sew those delicate flowers and vines
      or was it someone else?
Or the knitted forest green dress Helga Howie gave you
      sold for a thousand dollars, in 1972
      one of the hems unraveling, a minor defect
      she was an impulsive woman, like many artists
      so she gave the dress to you.

Or the sweater with the belt and the reindeer
    you still a teen when you began to wear it.
And the trench coat that you wore in the Shasta Road days
On the day you took BART to the city, to audition for Mignon
you wore that coat.

MARGARET JENKINS PERFORMANCE
Part Three

Waltz turns, peasant musurkas
   Duncan dance looks deceptively simple.
Movement originating from the sternum, a leading
   and a flowering from the heart.
Wearing Grecian tunics made of silk
   you are temple dancers, dancing to the music of
   Chopin, Brahms, Gluck, Tchaikovsky, Schubert.
There were four of you dancing that night
   on a rainy evening at the Margaret Jenkins Studio
   January 1982.

Nancy was the star, with her San Francisco Ballet training
   Maria with her perfect body
   Melinda, dark and dramatic
   but behind it all, in your understated way
   you were the quiet conductor
   I don't think any of them would dispute that.
You were the one who sensed
   when the choreography didn't quite match the music
   an almost imperceptible change in footwork
   restoring the balance between music and gesture
   you are brilliant in that way.
You might say 'don't worry about the steps
   dance from inside the music, be the music
   it's not about memorizing steps'.
You – the angel of obliteration is your best friend
   yet you were the glue that held it all together
   I've given up trying to understand.

With a performance of this magnitude there are
    thousands of choices—
    should Nancy be paired with Melinda or Maria
    which tunic should be worn for the Gluck
    a musical prelude before the first dance
    or should we just begin?
What about refreshments, or ticket sales, and what about publicity
    and then there is the order of the dances
    what to start with, and which one will be the finale?
Each choice by itself might seem relatively minor
    but if there's a brick loose in the foundation
    temple of the moment could come crashing down.
The DDD's were the very essence of a collective
    input of each dancer honored and considered
    yet my dear, they all knew it and I know it too
    the Gods were whispering in your ear.

1st half - all
white tunics)   Costumes

		Basic	Accessories
1)	Andante & Scherzo —	white	Multi scarves
2)	Orientale —	" (put on scarf)	?
3)	Water —	" (put on scarf)	?
4)	Flames —	*(K & M could change here)	
5)	Gypsy (Mario's yellow as overtune?) —	white (no time to change before G.V.)	2 scarves (take off for G.V.)
6)	Grande Valse —	white only	~~scarves~~
7)	D + M	white	wreath + scarf
8)	Rose Petals —	white only	~~scarves~~ + petals
9)	Dubin —	red	— chains
10)	Scriabin —	red	— ?
11)	Varsavianka —	red	— tattered sash
12)	Destiny —	?	
13)	Satie —	?	
14)	Furies —	cape	— tights + leotards
15)	Bl. Spirits —	Greek tunic	
16)	Priestess —	" "	
17)	Air (in) —	" "	
18)	Bacchanale —	" "	ivy wreaths

THE REAL YOU

Oh my dear, I fumble and hesitate
   trying to get it right
   above all else I want to fit in.

But my darling, you are a queen
   you have no interest in fitting in
   you want to be left alone.
After all, queens live a solitary, private life
   queens are above the rest of us
   queens are complete within themselves.

Oh I wonder what it was like for you
   when you saw your first Byrne-Jones
   or Rosetti, or especially Alta-Tadema
   must have been a bolt of lightning
   for a young girl growing up in the suburbs
   suddenly the face of truth.
Or that night your great aunt took you to the Opera House
   you were just a child then, a little girl of five
   but already your own person.

Yours is a language of temples and palaces and marble
   for you the realm of the imagination more real than reality.
You are the most present person I know.
And the interstellar black of your absence
   is your midsummer golden nimbus
   somehow flipped around, turned inside out.
What other explanation can there be, for what you've become?
   unclean, unwashed, your cashmere sweaters ripped and torn
   the horrible sore eating away your face.

Oh my dear, you are that temple
  of marble and banners and summer sun
  on a bluff overlooking the vast Pacific
  and that will never change.
  Where the music of the morning star
  lives inside the balmy breeze.
And we dance with you, and for you
  a dance of roses and youthful hopes
  born of the love birthed in the tension between sun and moon.
More than noble, more than glorious
  are the notes of the earth and sky
  as played by the court musicians on their gilded horns.
And as we listen, we bow down
  overwhelmed by more than we can understand
  as we watch the rhythms of the planting and the harvest
  within your sacred dance.

You are a decomposition, a breaking down and a rotting
  the fertility of the in between.
And yet, your faith in me remains unchanged.
Sometimes I think you need all that darkness
  to better sense your golden light.
And in spite of all my shortcomings
  you faithfully hold my most perfect self.
And please, don't even try to forgive yourself
  please let the rest of us do that for you
  we will carry that rose to the end of our hours
  and our hearts will be forever gladdened.

HIDDEN HELPER

You live in the mythic realm
maybe the angel of death is your helper
or perhaps it's the other way around.
You live in the mythic realm, you were
and still are true to your mythic roots
more real for you than flesh and bones
'till death do us part'.

Outwardly you are so like your father
   extremely smart, extremely quiet
   extremely careful with your words.
Except for you it's just a game
   you could play that game in your sleep.
Everyday stuff of no consequence for you
   You, who are faithful to your wine.

Obliteration can be the falling of a leaf
   coyote stalking quail
   Kali mischief … what did Oppenheimer say,
   after the first successful test?
   "…if the light of a thousand suns were to burst in the sky
   then… I am death, the shatterer of worlds"

Yes the angel of Death is here, for you, even for me
She holds you, kisses you good morning.
She teaches you your waltz turns
   which you teach to your students
   is that where you got your rhythm?
Good to erase, erase the slate, tabala rasa.

First obliterate, then start anew is how I imagine it
    don't ever think that the mythic realm is just an idea
    or some sort of imagining
    for the mythic realm is more real than your jugular vein.

Qu'est-ce Que C'est, my darling, why
    are you not stirring?
I shake your shoulder, but you do not open your eyes.
You always did prefer to be left alone
    do you still remember my name?

MARGARET JENKINS PERFORMANCE
Part Four

The evening created its own momentum
    deepening, ever deepening into the soul of each piece.
The audience often quiet, but as the dances unfolded,
    one after another
    stillness of the pond thickening into applause.
    We all felt it
    like a ripple or a pulse reconfiguring into a portal
    an invocation to the spirits
    and they came, the spirits were there that night
    inside the Margaret Jenkins Studio
    the four of you brought them to all of us
    with your movement, your gestures, your offerings
    after forty years that night ripples inside me still.

Dance can be thought of as a collection of gestures.
Gestures so quick they capture the invisible
    for an instant, less than an instant
    a firefly flash in the in-between
    a tuning, a remedy, a resonance.
Most of the dances performed that night were short
    five or seven or eight minutes.
A common misperception is that Duncan dance is improvised
    the construction of the dance has it looking fresh and spontaneous.
Much of the choreography from Mignon
    she spent a few years as a young woman
    in Isadora's school in Russia
    late 20s I believe.

You call yourselves the Dionysian Duncan Dancers
    DDD's for short.
And Chris, that name was your inspiration
    ironic in a way
    I can't imagine anyone less Dionysian than you.
You come from a place of palaces and aristocracy
    you never change
    I can't imagine anyone more at ease with themselves than you.
You are a living paradox, you wear your silence and enigma
    like a favorite coat.

And sometimes, with a few of the dances
    Mignon's version differed slightly from Irma's, or Maria-Theresa's.
Because you are so musical, and have the capacity to fully submit
    the spirit of the music bleeds into you
    you might say 'these steps work a little better'
    for releasing the dove inside the gesture.
The others rarely questioned you
    your 'rightness' not so much about an idea or concept
    more like a direct perception
    offered back like a golden sparkle by the wisdom of the moment.

* Problems   Entrances / Exits / ~~Costumes~~

Pre-curtain : all in costume stage left for Andante entrance

1) Andante & Scherzo (ALL) Enter: stage left   Exit: stage right

2) Orientale   (Karen) Enter: stage right   Exit: stage right

3) Water   (Linda) Enter: stage right   Exit : [stage left]

4) Flames   (Karen & Maria) Enter: stage right   Exit ~~stage left~~ stage right

* 5) Gypsy   (Chris) Enter: stage right Exit [stage left]

6) Grande Valse   (Chris + Linda) Enter: stage left | Chris exit stage right
                  (Karen + Maria) Enter : stage right | Karen exit stage right
                                      cross exit | Maria exit [stage left]
                                        leap | Linda exit [stage left]

7) Death + Maiden (M)   Enter: [Stage Left]   Exit: [Stage left]

8) Rose Petals   ~~Karen~~
                 (Chris + Karen) Enter stage right
                 (Linda + Maria) Enter stage left

---

9) Dubinushka   (All) enter: stage right (All) exit: stage right

10) Scriabin   (Karen) enter: stage right exit: stage right

11) Varsavianka   (All) enter : stage right   (All) exit : stage right

12) Destiny   (3) enter : stage right   (3) exit : stage right

13) Satie   (M) enter : stage right   (M) exit : stage right

14) Furies   (All) enter : stage right   (All) exit: stage right

15) Bl. Spirits   (All) enter : stage right   (All) exit: stage right
                     * C.M. stay on stage ?)   (M) exit : stage right

16) Priestess

17) Air Gai   (All) enter: stage right   (All) exit: stage right
                     * (transition)

18) Bacchanale

All entrances & exits for 2nd half. All entrances & exits stage right

46

THE PATH CURLS BACK ON ITSELF

Why the grief?
I'm losing Chris, but I'm also losing myself.
Spiritual life is found in this world
    not in any other place, only here
    this body, my body
    this ground, my ground.
I can't find myself, and I am running out of time
    yet the weakness I feel, my incompleteness
    those are pieces of God as well
    I know in my heart I will never get there.

You won't even see my footprints
    I keep wandering down the animal paths
    where only the lost boys go
    I keep looking for the parts of my heart
    that I must have mislaid somewhere
    keep looking for those lost little beads of life
    that I bartered away in some fools bargain
    please help me, for I have lost my way.

WITH ALAN

You lived your life backwards. You came here as a sophisticate
    even as a child you had refined tastes.
And you leave in rags
    sleeping in your piss.

I remember only a few years ago, at the Opera House
you saw Alan, the Chronicle's dance critic
    you said 'oh, there's Alan', like he was your best friend.
    Sore on your face stinking like a corpse
    you had five glasses of wine on an empty stomach
    the wine only made you stronger.

The two of you were talking
    in a language only a few could understand
    of syncopations and entrances
    tension inside a gesture.
You see the world differently than the rest of us
    chandeliers of your royal court cast no shadow.

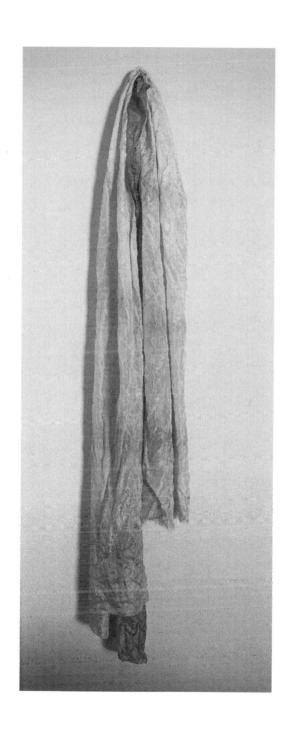

LIKE A MAGICAL LITTLE ANIMAL

Oh I like the dry wind, dry air
the wind brings me such depth, as if the depth isn't mine
the wind brings it to me, offers it to me.

Maybe the wind helps me re-collect all the pieces
    I live too much in the in-between
    I'm in the dream, but I'm looking for depth
    I'm looking to find myself
    depth is like a root
    a taproot, my taproot.

The last time we had coffee together, we went to the Rose Garden
Dry air, early morning, the weather changing
I felt it in the wind. A shift
    from east to west
    from the dawning to the twilight
    I'm open now, there's a hole in my stomach
    your hours are running out.

You follow behind, like a magical little animal
I look over my shoulder; you are so shaky.
You might fall, right in the middle of the street.
Strength is there for a few steps
    then the wobbling, the shaking.
You look at the soup, say
    'it doesn't look right', or
    'it doesn't smell right'

But you want to come with me
you want to say 'hi' to the people.

Into Peets, only a couple of people in line, still early.
We look at the banana bread, the blackberry scone
I ask you if they are OK
you say nothing
but later you nibble at the banana bread
it's too sweet, but calories are calories.

I wanted to go to the bench at Inspiration Point
but the park is closed because of the fire danger.
So we drive to the Rose Garden instead.

MARGARET JENKINS PERFORMANCE
Part Five

The DDD's opened that night with the Dubinshka—
    dubina is Russian for soul, or soul forces.
    And isn't the Russian soul held by the peasants
    with their intimate connection with the land?
Later, the Allegro Con Gratzia from Tchaikovsky's
    Pathetique symphony.
'Pathos', such an interesting word
    wounding and longing rolled up in a tangle
    before the great unknown
    but looking with a different set of eyes
    the eyes of the heart perhaps
    you notice that what looked like tangles
are branches of the great oak tree.
Suffering is like that
    suffering is pain before it is danced
    then it becomes the grandmother to compassion.

In the middle of the program, a series of dances
    from Gluck's opera, Orpheus and Eurydice.
Orpheus, the greatest musician in the land
    is in love with Eurydice, who is trapped
    in the underworld, a place of terror and haunting
    all who enter that dark and indistinct realm inevitably go mad.
But Orpheus goes down without a second thought
    his love for Eurydice keeps his soul intact
    trailing breadcrumbs as he searches for her.
And he finds her, the Lord of Death releases her to him
    no problem!
    The only condition is, that as they make their way

back to the realm of life, back to the world of night and day
he doesn't look back
if he looks back he will lose her forever.

But of course he does look back
while following the trail of breadcrumbs up to the light
there is a strange stirring inside
he's not sure if he can still feel her
not sure if she's still there.
So he takes a quick peek, to put his worries to rest
and in so doing, loses his love forever.

From earth to air, then ending with water
and you are the quiet and steady flame.
The evening ended with two dances to the music of Gluck
the ephemeral 'Dance of the Blessed Spirits'
and then the 'Bacchanale', a wild and festive
interweaving of music and movement.
When the music stopped, exhilaration and depth were in the air
people milled about, and even though we were strangers
we all felt like we knew each other.
For the evening of dance was an invocation
and stirred awake in me and so many of the others
the most alive part of myself
which is my heart.

I

Polonaise Militaire   Ensemble
  Chopin . . . . . . .Opus 40 #1

Dubinishka   Ensemble
  Traditional Russian Folksong

"The time has come and the people awoke,
Straightened their backs bent as long,
Shook themselves free of century-old burdens
And against its foes raised the 'dubina'."

Moment Musicale   Ensemble
  Schubert . . . .Opus 94 #5

(pause)

Allegro Con Grazia   Ensemble
  Tchaikovsky . . . . . Symphony #6 "Pathetique"

The dream of youth and love
A presentiment of sorrow to come.

Mazurka "Orientale"   Nancy
  Chopin . . . . . . Opus 68 #2

Gypsy   Ensemble
  Brahms . . . . Opus 39 #4

Flames   Ensemble
  Brahms . . . . Opus 39 #14

Moment Musicale   Maria
  Schubert . . . .Opus 94 #3

Water Dance   Melinda
  Schubert . . . .Opus 91 #12

Rose Petals   Ensemble
  Brahms . . . . Opus 39 #15

•••••••••• 15 Minute Intermission ••••••••••

II

THE OPERAS OF GLUCK

"Orpheus and Eurydice"

In this Greek myth Orpheus ventures to the underworld to find his beloved Eurydice. He first encounters the Furies, tortured souls of Hades. Eventually he reaches the Blessed Spirits. Moved by his music, they allow the two to reunite. Orpheus and Eurydice are freed from the underworld, provided Orpheus does not look back.

Dance of a Fury   Melinda

Dance of the Furies   Ensemble

Elysian Fields   Christina

(musical interlude)

Air   Christina, Maria

Gavotte   Ensemble

"Iphigenia In Aulis"

Iphigenia and Electra celebrate the departure of their father, King Agamemnon, and the Greek fleet bound for Troy. Their dance includes the ritual offering to the Gods. The Goddess Artemis is displeased and requires the sacrifice of Iphigenia to calm the stormy seas. When she agrees to die willingly, Iphigenia is sent instead to Tauris to serve as Priestess. Iphigenia implores the gods to free her from her sacrifical duties. By the grace of Athena, Iphigenia rejoins her sister and companions in a joyous celebration of Dionysus.

Air gai/Lento/Air gai   Maria, Nancy

Bacchanal   Ensemble

CASHMERE SWEATERS

Like taking a big exhale, so you can inhale more deeply
like the angel of death pushing down on your back body
    'you need to completely empty out'
    so you can submit to the next breath.
    Full, enriching, life-giving next breath.

Why such radical measures? All this Marxist-Leninist—
    that's not really you, that's so far away from you.
    You were never a worker, always the queen
    you had that glow, like a medieval painting
    that mid-summer evening glow.
Even when it got really bad, with your ripped clothes
    and unwashed body
    you were part of the fairy realm
    even the angelic realm.

What does the self get transformed into
through the atom bomb of obliteration?
You are an extremist, in your own way of course.
Those communists, those socialists, they were beneath you
Their love of the proletariat — you were never proletariat
    yet you tolerated me.

Been going through your clothes, my dear
    cashmere, silk, even cashmere pants
    linen for summertime, high quality cotton, Scottish wool.
Piles of clothes, in boxes, milk cartons, or just piled in the corner
    you never put anything away.

Worn for months at a time, then discarded
  you'd buy something new
  cashmere sweater, honey colored
  wooden buttons, or mother of pearl
  which you'd wear until the rips appear
  riddled with holes, piled up by your bed
  silk blouses, endless cashmere, what am I going to do with them?
 What would you have me do?

You never planned ahead, you trusted that the world would provide
  yet you never trusted yourself
  obliteration — like a rip in the fabric of time.

I trusted you, though you must have found me boring.
You never said much, yet you supported my crazy ideas
  my little insecurities and avoidances.
You are grounded in so many ways
  sophisticated
  you, who know more Duncan choreography than anyone alive
  you believed in me
  how could you not believe in yourself?

At least you're eating now.
At least I can place a chunk of banana bread by you
as you lie in your bed.
You don't respond, you don't look up
a hand reaches out, you break the bread apart
stuff the pieces in your mouth without opening your eyes
without sitting up.
qu'est-ce que c'est, my dear, you're lying in crumbs!

CRANBERRIES

Oh that last day
   seems like any other day
   trapped by the silence, I take small breaths
   I'm not sure I know what to do
   not sure if I should show my face.

But you wanted something with cranberries
   a scone or a muffin.
Why cranberries? But I don't ask
I go to the french bakery on Solano, across from Peet's
   for a cranberry scone, loaded with sugar
   baked almost crispy — you might like that
   is what I'm thinking.

A hand reaches out from under the covers
   when I return with the scone.
You never show your face; you don't eat the scone
   you pick the cranberries out
   like a bird picking at seeds
   I never did see your face.

And I remember thanksgiving dinners
   that your father cooked, thirty years ago.
   His name was Orton, he was a Swede
   he never did like me all that well.
Turkey dinner, with stuffing, mashed potatoes, gravy
   cranberries on a silver serving tray.
Cranberries, with their slightly tart taste
   give form, definition, to the gravy, white meat, stuffing.

Spiritual life is an opening, a renewing, a refreshening
   and grief is the contrast.
A door that has been open for most of my life
   now closed, never to open again.
   Never noticed the door until it was gone
   never noticed the door, but I feel its absence.

CORRIDORS OF SILENCE

We're all ghosts in a way
  we cling to what we know
  or to the people we encounter along the way.
Life has become uncertain, it flickers on and off
  precipitates into a shape before dissolving
  like fireflies winking bright in the night—
  just when you think to look
  the light already has slipped away.
  Our world has become a place
  indistinct, ephemeral and vague.

Dreams are so powerful, they can suck you in.
Through grief, the heart finds her definition
  like the tide pulling out in the twilight hour
  seashells spinning in the glistening sand
  grief can give a life its clarity
  even its substance.

We walked through our corridors of silence, you and I
  that most holy church of the everyday
  you and I both drawn to the dark and the hidden
  we are so similar in that way.
Yet I always thought it all led somewhere
  some sort of purpose, or higher plan.
But you never grasped for much of anything.
And now, just quietly lying with your eyes closed
  day by day, month by month, a year and a half now
  you seem certain of your way.
I guess hearts are meant to be broken
  when you lose what you cannot bear to lose
  is when you begin to assemble the pieces of yourself.

DIONYSIAN DUNCAN DANCERS

Margaret Jenkins Perfomance Space
San Francisco

Friday, January 22, 1982
Saturday, January 23, 1982

Van Deering Perrine

Drawing from the cover used for all
of Isadora Duncan's 1921 Russian
concerts' programs.

MARGARET JENKINS PERFORMANCE
Part Six

I shouldn't make too much of that night
  40 years ago now, a night only a few will remember.
But at the time the DDD's were on the Bay Area's cultural radar.
  And the two performances at Margaret Jenkins studio
  resonated for months through San Francisco's art world.
People were talking and people were listening
  even Alan Ulrich, the Examiner's extremely picky dance critic
  wrote a detailed and favorable review.
Even though Isadora's artistic career had its home in Europe
  she was born in San Francisco, and perhaps because of that
  the spirit of Isadora throughout the last hundred years
  is in powerful synchronous resonance
  with San Francisco's beat poet, Buddhist, left coast, human
  be-in, City Lights.
  Haight Ashbury, Trips Festival, soul.
In the 60s and early 70s, with the incredible music scene
  at the Fillmore and Avalon—
  a Dionysian scene if there ever was one—
  renewed an interest in Isadora Duncan dance.
  Because they adhered carefully to the traditions of
  Duncan dance
  and because they could capture the radicalism
  and the innocence of this life-affirming dance
  the DDD's rode that wave for several years.

But you never talk about the Margaret Jenkins performance
  in the last 40 years you never mentioned it
  not even once.

I visit you in your care facility
    I bring you your scone, your cappuccino
    you sit up, we work on the puzzles together
    I read to you from spiritual books.
But still you don't speak, all you do is sleep
    you're still a queen—the queen
    in her very small world, tiny white-washed room
    like Eurydice, removed from this disappointing and
    suffering world.
Maybe it's better to wipe the slate clean
Maybe it's better to obliterate the past
    maybe its better to not have roots
    not have a future.
You are a genius, and I'm so predictably ordinary
    who am I to say?

Maybe its better in the realm of the timeless
    day-to-day life never gets anywhere
    I might be the biggest fool who ever lived
    thinking I'm gonna find an all encompassing purpose.
Maybe I'm just feeding myself delusions so I can get by
    survive another day
    survive myself.
Maybe my innocence is a fragment of a dream
    that keeps curling back on itself
    because I can't open my eyes.
But honey, please listen to me for once
    I need to stay here, in the realm of life
    I've already carried your grief.

You might be one of people who come here
    and give your gifts clean and quick
    a firefly wink and then your are gone

back to your home in the stars.
Many artists are like that; Isadora for one
    Chopin, Schumann, Keats, maybe Rilke
    Simone Weil, Jimi Hendrix, even Jerry Garcia
    they all left before their time
    they made their offering, then split the scene.
They molded and shaped the Beautiful
    then they slipped out the back door.
Like you have, my dear, I'm not sure you would dispute that.
The county nurse called it
    one of the worst cases of self-neglect she had ever seen.
But what you left behind for the rest of us
    is Beauty, is Love
    wild, innocent, uncorrupted.

But then, as I was doing my research
    before writing this piece
    I asked you if you had a program from that night
    I looked a little bit, but couldn't find one.
You told me you did, but it was in your purse.
But everything you had: your clothes, your collection of books
    your phone and of course your purse
    you lost all that when the care facility burned down
    you don't react at all when you tell me that
    you just look at me, blue eyes unblinking
    like its less than nothing
    as I turn away to hide my tears.

Love is the Way of Weakness

Most feel like they are growing into their more perfect selves
    yet, over time, the wounds can deepen as well.
Inside your unique and precious wound
    might be where your beauty is found.
When the foundations of whoever it is
    that you think you are
    break and crumble –
    that's when you fall
    you know when you're falling because it really hurts
    that's when, if you're lucky
    you fall into yourself.

My dear, you are doing better at the new care facility
    where they placed you
    after the first one burned down.
Often I go to see you – I'll go later today
    after I scratch out these words.
I look forward to seeing you
    although it's a bit of a drive.
You're looking better, they keep you clean
    you're eating now, putting on some weight
We do puzzles, I read to you
    not much to say, we've known each other so long
    most of our communication is silent.
I turn out the light when it's time to leave
    you roll over, go back to sleep.

You were never much for struggling
    you let me do the struggling.
And while I could say that you are really good at hiding—
    for you as the golden girl
    you hid inside your perfect self.
But it must also be said
    that you are the most honest person
    you can be trusted to give the truth.
In the end, the truth for all of us
    is that everything we think we have will be taken away
    except for what lives in our heart.

Love is the way of weakness.

RIPPLE

Or some other density
    a concentration, a locus of forces
    a hardening and a releasing
    a husking, and a scattering of seeds

Inside my absence is a woman
    stardust
    morphs into a shape.
Even the briefest glance
    an evaporating into space
    a dissolving, yet the image
    echos inside me
    a rippling across my hidden lake

as I twist her crystalline wisdom
    into the vortex of my days.
I can be absent too
    in the caverns of some other place.
These are strange days
    in the sticky spiderweb of life.
Animals flee the inferno forest
    bloated fish wash up on the stony shore.

And as my clods and irregular forms tumble and fall
    please touch my blood
    with your mercy and grace.
As I struggle to see through the panes
    I never did see all that well
    but I'll never forget the lines of your face.

THE DIONYSIAN DUNCAN DANCERS

Perform a legacy of original dances choreographed by

ISADORA DUNCAN

Saturday   November 22, 1980
8 p.m.
Sunset Center Theater
Carmel, California

Thursday   December 18, 1980
8 p.m.
Louden Nelson Community Theater
301 Center Street
Santa Cruz, California

Tickets at the door: $5.00 General Admission; $3.50 Students/Seniors

The Dionysian Duncan Dancers are the performing company of The Isadora Duncan International
Institute of Classical Dance (415) 673-3581.

there will always be a stitch
in the sacred fabric
even if you never come back.

THANKS TO:

Jane Brunette *for the design and layout of this collection, and for her capacity to imagine the wholeness of what I am trying to do better than I do.*

Katrin Arefy, my writing partner via Zoom when I created most of these poems, for her insightful feedback and overall support during a difficult time.

Andy Couturier, my writing mentor and unflagging encourager.

Brian Fessenden for all his help with the photographs.

Copyright © 2021 by Bruce Fessenden. All rights reserved.
ISBN 978-0-9892605-6-5
Published by flamingseed press. flamingseed.com

Made in the USA
Columbia, SC
27 September 2021

45721133R00039